Take a Little Time for Yourself

ARTWORK BY

Kathy Hatch

HARVEST HOUSE PUBLISHERS

EUGENE, OREGON

Take a Little Time for Yourself
Copyright * 2007 by Harvest House Publishers
Eugene, Oregon 97402

ISBN-13: 978-0-7369-1972-2
ISBN-10: 0-7369-1972-4

Design and production by Koechel Peterson & Associates, Inc., Minneapolis, Minnesota

For even when the time comes and you
can relax, you hardly know how.
◦◦ Alice Foote MacDougall ◦◦

There are simply *too many* things in our lives to stress us out. *Fortunately*, there are just as many things that can make us happy. We *simply* have to take the time to notice them and bring them into our *lives*.

 AUTHOR UNKNOWN

There is a time for everything,
and a season for every activity under heaven.
ECCLESIASTES 3:1

Puttering is really a time to be alone, to dream and to get
in touch with yourself.... To putter is to discover.

∞ Alexandra Stoddard ∞

Orange & Tangerine Bath Soak

INGREDIENTS:

½ cup baking soda

¼ cup Epsom salts

2 drops orange food coloring

10 drops orange essential oil

10 drops tangerine essential oil

INSTRUCTIONS:

Combine all ingredients in a bowl and stir
until color is evenly distributed.
Transfer mixture into a food processor
and grind into a fine powder.
Spoon into a bottle or jar for storage.

USE:
Add 3-4 tablespoons
to warm bath.

When in doubt, *take a bath*.

It can *calm* your mind,

relax your tired, tense body,

and soothe your stressed *soul*.

Baths are as necessary for spiritual *replenishment*

and centering as are *prayer* and meditation.

SARAH BAN BREATHNACH

Finish each day and be done with it.
You have done what you could.
Tomorrow is a new day; begin it well and serenely
and with too high a spirit
to be encumbered with your old nonsense.

RALPH WALDO EMERSON

True silence
is the rest of the mind; it is
to the spirit what sleep is to the body:
nourishment and refreshment.

WILLIAM PENN

Purposely quiet your mind with a period of relaxation before going to bed. Dim the lights early, turn off the television, stay away from your computer, and avoid reading anything thought provoking. This may seem obvious, but for years I stimulated my mind with inspirational books before trying to go to sleep. Ambitious planning or problem-solving right up until bedtime will keep you awake. Instead, fill your evenings with soft music and easy reading....

Try taking a warm bath, lighting a candle, and listening to the same soothing music each night (the secret to rituals is repetition). Choose something comfortable to lounge in, sip a steamy cup of herbal tea, and offer up a good-night prayer of thanksgiving. Just before lights-out, tell yourself that you will have a restful night's sleep and that tomorrow is brimming with wonderful opportunities. Quiet the inner voice that tempts you to concentrate on the obstacles of today or the limitations and uncertainties of tomorrow. Focus on the solutions and possibilities that will come after a good night's rest.   Sweet dreams!

SUE AUGUSTINE
5-Minute Retreats for Women

Peace is not something you wish for;
It's something you make,
Something you do,
Something you are,
And something you give away.

ROBERT FULGHUM

It is important to have friends,
   but it is important to truly
      get to know the person
   you will be spending
the rest of your life with:
yourself. And the only way
to do this is to… spend time
with yourself, learn what
makes you happy. There is
always something, and once
you find it, you have the
key to a content life.
Once that is done, your
busy days will end not in
exhaustion, but exhilaration.

NATHAN HUNSTAD

Lavender
SOAP BALLS

2 bars soap (unscented vegetable-based)
½ cup dried lavender blossoms
5 drops lavender essential oil
¼ cup warm water

INSTRUCTIONS:

Using a cheese grater, grate soap bars into a large bowl.
Add the lavender blossoms. Add the lavender
essential oil and mix thoroughly. Add warm
water and stir again. Roll heaping tablespoons of
mixture into balls. Place on cookie sheet and allow
to air dry completely for 2–3 days.

Treat a Friend

Place several Soap Balls in soap dish,
wrap with lavender tulle and tie closed with
pretty ribbon and a sprig of lavender.

Spend time each day talking
with your friends.
Even a 15~ or 20~minute
conversation can help reduce stress,
create emotional bonds,
and give objective insights.

∞ Pepper Schwartz, Ph.D. ∞

LAVENDER

LAVENDER

Rest is not idleness,
and to lie
sometimes on the
grass under the
trees on a
summer's day,
listening to the
murmur of water,
or watching
the clouds float across
the sky, is by no means
a waste of time.

JOHN LUBBOCK

14

The joy of spirit indicates its strength. All healthy things are sweet tempered.

Sleep, nature's rest,

divine tranquility,

That brings *peace* to

the mind.

Ovid

RELAXING LAVENDER
Salt Crystals

INGREDIENTS:

1 cup borax (desert salt)

2 cups Epsom salts

½ cup coarse sea salt

¼ cup baking soda

¼ cup white clay

½ cup dried lavender buds

10 drops lavender essential oil

INSTRUCTIONS:

In large bowl, mix together
the borax, salts, baking
soda and clay. Crush the dried
lavender flowers and whisk into salt mix.
Add essential oil and mix thoroughly with
wire whisk. Cover bowl with towel and allow to set
8–10 hours for scent to absorb. Mix thoroughly
again and package in glass jars. Makes 4 cups.

USE:

¼ to ½ cup in tub full
of warm water.

FOR GIFT GIVING:

Package in pretty jars,
cover jar lid with fabric,
wrap with raffia or
silk ribbon and include
instructions for use.

LAVENDER
Bath Salts

God had a purpose in ordering a Sabbath. In resting one day each week, women have time to enjoy their families and rejuvenate. In addition to rest on the Sabbath, I suggest a monthly dinner with friends, long walks, the occasional leisurely bubble bath, or other activities that offer a few hours' respite from the daily grind.

When your body begs to slow down but your schedule won't, remind yourself that you also have the responsibility to take care of you. So take time…to pamper yourself. You deserve it.

LISA TUTTLE

Bubble Bath

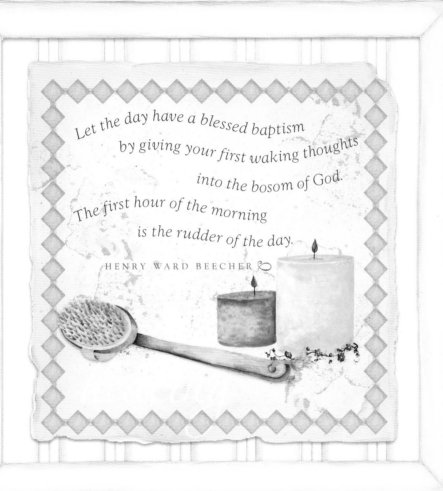

Let the day have a blessed baptism
by giving your first waking thoughts
into the bosom of God.
The first hour of the morning
is the rudder of the day.

HENRY WARD BEECHER

19

All the **wonders**
that you seek
are within **yourself.**

SIR THOMAS BROWN

*Every day brings a chance for you
to draw in a breath,
kick off your shoes, and dance.*

•• Oprah Winfrey ••

Hot **BATHS** 25¢

The minute you settle
for less than you deserve,
you get even less
than you settle for.

MAUREEN DOWD

21

Ocean Blue Bubbling Bath Gel

INGREDIENTS:

1 cup water
¼ cup fresh chamomile
3 drops jasmine essential oil
4 drops vanilla essential oil
2 tablespoons liquid glycerin
5 tablespoons grated castile soap
1 tablespoon unflavored gelatin
1 drop blue food coloring

INSTRUCTIONS:

Boil the water and make an infusion with the
chamomile and boiling water. Grate the castile soap.
Strain the herb infusion and discard herbs.
Add the soap and liquid glycerin to water and stir well.
Add essential oils and food coloring, stirring
again. Add the gelatin last and stir until it is fully
dissolved. Allow mixture to cool and
transfer to small glass jars.

USE:

Add 3-4 tablespoons under running tub water
for a luxurious scented bath!

GIFT GIVING:

Transfer gel to small decorative glass container,
tie pretty fabric over lid, secure with ribbon and add
directions for use on label or hang tag.

Makes about 1 pint of gel

I believe the nicest and sweetest days are not those on which anything very splendid or wonderful or exciting happens, but just those that bring simple little pleasures, following one another softly, like pearls slipping off a string.

LUCY M. MONTGOMERY
Anne of Green Gables

The still beauty of dawn is nature's finest balm.
∞ Edwin Way Teale ∞

Year by year the *complexities*
of this spinning world
grow more bewildering,
and so each year
we need all the more
to seek *peace* and *comfort*
in the joyful simplicities.

AUTHOR UNKNOWN

Rest when you're weary. Refresh
and renew yourself, your body,
your mind, your spirit.
Then get back to work.

RALPH MARSTON

Lemon Herbal
Facial Steam

INGREDIENTS:

2 quarts water
1 cup dried chamomile
¼ cup fresh lemon juice

Bring water and lemon juice to boil in large pot.
Add chamomile flowers, cover, and remove from heat.
Wait 2 minutes — uncover and stir.

Being solitary is being alone well:
being alone luxuriously immersed in
doings of your own choice.

∞ Alice Koller ∞

Place pot on a protective surface and at
a height where you can sit comfortably
with face 6" above pot. Drape a
large towel over your head and
sides of pot. Relax and allow
steam to clean and open
facial pores for 10–15 minutes.

luxurious

Solitude is such a potential thing.
We hear voices in solitude
we never hear in the hurry and
turmoil of life; we receive
counsels and comforts we get
under no other condition.

AMELIA E. BARR

TAKE TIME

Take time to think
  It is the source of all power.
Take time to play
  It is the secret of perpetual youth.
Take time to read
  It is the fountain of wisdom.
Take time to pray
  It is the greatest power on earth.
Take time to love and be loved
  It is a God-given privilege.
Take time to be friendly
  It is the road to happiness.
Take time to laugh
  It is the music of the soul.
Take time to give
  It is too short a day to be selfish.
Take time to work
  It is the price of success.

AUTHOR UNKNOWN

Once we *learn* to accept
and cherish our need for solitude,
opportunities will arrive in which
we can learn to nourish our imaginations
and *nurture* our souls.

SARAH BAN BREATHNACH

The moments of happiness we enjoy
take us by surprise.
It is not that we seize them,
but that they seize us.

ASHLEY MONTAGU

True beauty dwells in deep retreats,

Whose veil is unremoved,

Till *heart* with heart in concord beats,

And the lover is *beloved.*

William Wordsworth

There are many things in life
that will catch your eye,
but only a few will catch your
heart...pursue those.

◦◦ Author Unknown ◦◦

Private Garden

SHOWERS

SOAP & TOWEL INCLUDED $1

I am a strong believer in women taking the time to self-nurture. I try to take ten minutes in the shower as I am getting ready for my day. It is my time for me and I think and reflect.

LISA LESLIE

Refreshing Herbal Footbath

COLLECT 2 CUPS EACH:
fresh chamomile, lavender, sage, and lemon balm

Steep herbs in 1 quart of boiling water.
Strain the herbs from the liquid and whisk in
1 tablespoon of grated unscented castile soap.
Pour into large basin and add more warm
water if necessary to fill bowl.
Add a few drops of lavender and chamomile
essential oils.

Soak feet for at least 10 minutes.
Pat them dry and massage in lavender scented
moisturizing foot cream. Put on a pair of clean
cotton socks and prop up feet on raised pillow.

Pamper yourself into wellness with little indulgences.
∞ Sue Augustine ∞

If women were convinced that a *day off* or an hour of solitude was a reasonable *ambition*, they would find a way of *attaining* it. As it is, they feel so unjustified in their demand that they rarely make the *attempt.*

ANNE MORROW LINDBERGH

Sometimes the most urgent thing you can possibly do is take a complete rest.

ASHLEIGH BRILLIANT

HERBAL scented BATHS

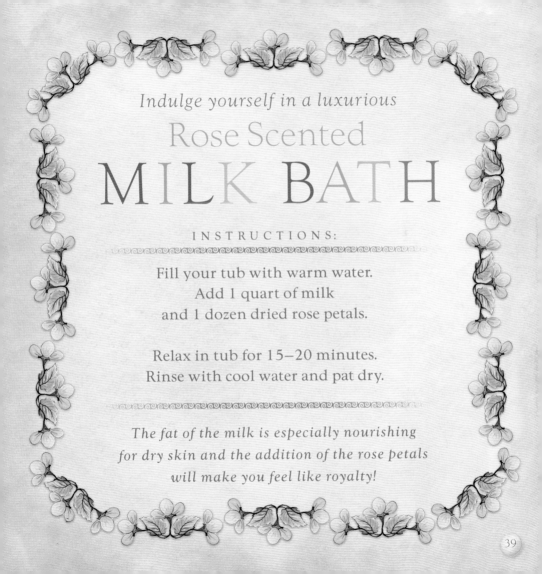

Indulge yourself in a luxurious

Rose Scented

MILK BATH

INSTRUCTIONS:

Fill your tub with warm water.
Add 1 quart of milk
and 1 dozen dried rose petals.

Relax in tub for 15–20 minutes.
Rinse with cool water and pat dry.

*The fat of the milk is especially nourishing
for dry skin and the addition of the rose petals
will make you feel like royalty!*

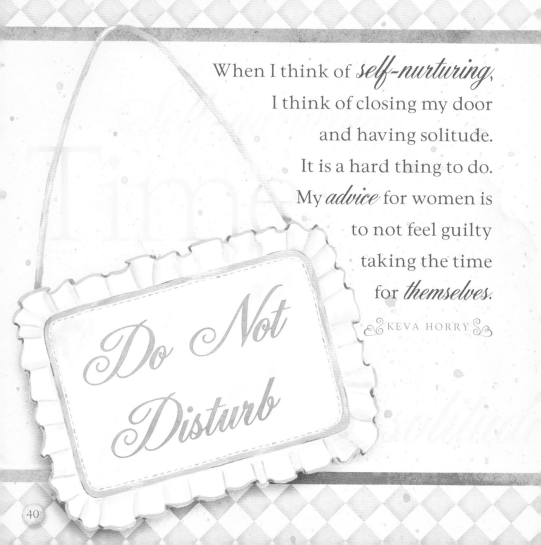

When I think of *self-nurturing,*
I think of closing my door
and having solitude.
It is a hard thing to do.
My *advice* for women is
to not feel guilty
taking the time
for *themselves.*

KEVA HORRY

Do Not Disturb

Take one hour of
alone time every day.
In addition to taking
time out, make
sure that you take
time to be by yourself,
and take a break
from everyone else.

DR. SUSAN LOVE

Bath Bags

INGREDIENTS:

½ cup regular oatmeal

½ cup powdered milk

4 tablespoons almond meal

16 drops strawberry essential oil

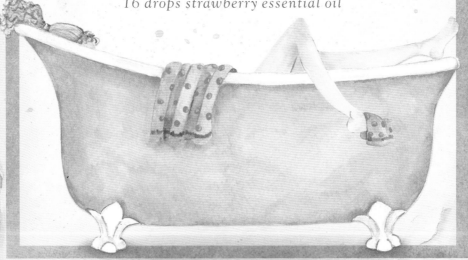

INSTRUCTIONS:

In bowl, thoroughly mix together dry ingredients.
Add essential oil and blend well. Divide mixture
into small muslin bags and tie closed with pretty ribbon.

Hang from bathtub faucet while
water is running into tub.

Being happy
doesn't mean that
everything is perfect.
It means that you've decided
to look beyond the imperfections.

AUTHOR UNKNOWN

43

You owe it to yourself
and those you love
to take good care
of your most valuable
resource—you!

MICHAEL ANGIER

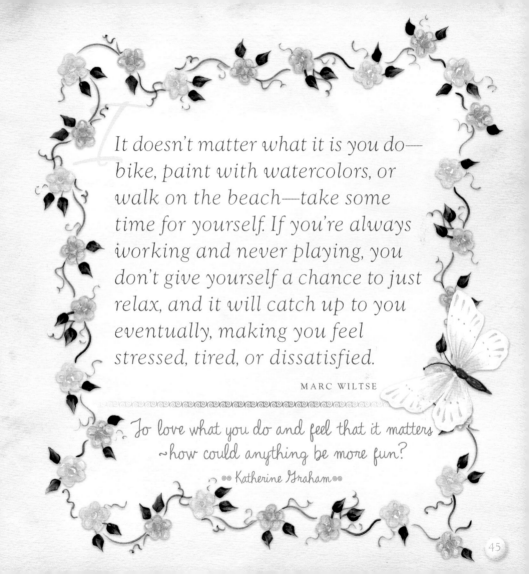

It doesn't matter what it is you do—bike, paint with watercolors, or walk on the beach—take some time for yourself. If you're always working and never playing, you don't give yourself a chance to just relax, and it will catch up to you eventually, making you feel stressed, tired, or dissatisfied.

MARC WILTSE

To love what you do and feel that it matters ~how could anything be more fun?

∞ Katherine Graham ∞

45

"How shall we beguile the lazy time if not with some delight?"
◦◦ William Shakespeare ◦◦

We act as though comfort and *luxury* were the chief **requirements** of life, when all that we need to make us *happy* is something to be *enthusiastic* about.

Charles Kingsley

47

Some of us need regular, *brief retreats* to quench our spiritual yearning. We need the quiet time to commune with the *sacred* as much as we need to eat and *sleep*.

RACHEL HARRIS

48

A successful day: to learn something
new; to laugh at least ten times;
to lift someone up; to make
progress on a worthy goal;
to practice peace and
patience; to do
something nice for
yourself and another; to
appreciate and be grateful
for all your blessings.

AUTHOR UNKNOWN

How you spend your time defines who you are.

OPRAH WINFREY

49

It's something
I've learned before, but
seem to have to relearn
over and over in different
circumstances—to help
others, you have to take
care of yourself.

MICHAEL ANGIER

Bath Oil

Learn to enjoy your own company.
You are the one person you can count on
living with for the rest of your life.

ANN RICHARDS

51

In solitude we give
passionate attention
to our lives, to our
memories, to the
details around us.

~ VIRGINIA WOOLF ~

Deliberately seeking solitude ~ quality
time spent away from family and
friends ~ may seem selfish. It is not.
Solitude is as necessary for our
creative spirits to develop and flourish
as are sleep and food for our bodies.

•• Sarah Ban Breathnach ••

FACIALS

FACIALS

Be gentle
with yourself.

MAX EHRMANN

MANICURE SET

BLUSH
PINK

*Nail
Polish*

ROSE
PINK

*Nail
Polish*

Play so that you may be serious.

ANACHARSIS ✑

Take 15 minutes every day to recall

the reasons that you believe in *yourself.*

Take the time to be *kind* and

generous to yourself, and then to others!

Miriam Nelson, Ph.D.

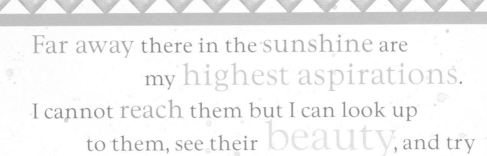

Far away there in the sunshine are
my highest aspirations.
I cannot reach them but I can look up
to them, see their beauty, and try
to follow where
they lead.

LOUISA MAY ALCOTT

Secret Garden Bath Tea

INGREDIENTS:

1 teaspoon dried lavender flowers
1 teaspoon dried rose petals
½ teaspoon dried lemon balm
¼ teaspoon dried rosemary
⅛ teaspoon dried spearmint
4 drops lavender essential oil
2 drops rose essential oil
1 drop patchouli essential oil
1 large heat sealable tea bag

*I will lie down
and sleep in peace.*

PSALM 4:8

56

INSTRUCTIONS:

Mix together dried ingredients.
Add essential oils and mix well. Fill heat sealable tea bag
with herb mix and seal.

It isn't the *big*
pleasures that count
the most; it's making
a great deal out of
the *little ones*.

⚬ JEAN WEBSTER ⚬

USE:

Add to tub while
filling with warm water.
Enjoy!

Open the door, let in the air;

The winds are *sweet* and the flowers are *fair*.

Joy is abroad in the world today;

If our door is wide, it may come this way.

Author Unknown

The best of all medicines is resting and fasting.

BENJAMIN FRANKLIN

Arranging a bowl of flowers
in the morning can give
a sense of quiet in a crowded day.

◦◦ Anne Morrow Lindbergh ◦◦

Plan one day a week to do something for yourself to nourish your soul. Use this time to remember your dreams and ideas. Schedule this day in your daybook.

DEB CHANEY

Body Wash

There are souls in this
world that have the
gift of finding
joy everywhere.

FREDERICK W. FABER

He who cannot rest
cannot work;
he who cannot let go
cannot hold on.
◦◦ Harry Emerson Fosdick ◦◦

HERBS

I am focused on finding ten minutes of my busy day for me.

It may be in the shower or a quick walk.

I have found that carving out that time is extremely important for me.

JUDGE GLENDA HATCHETT

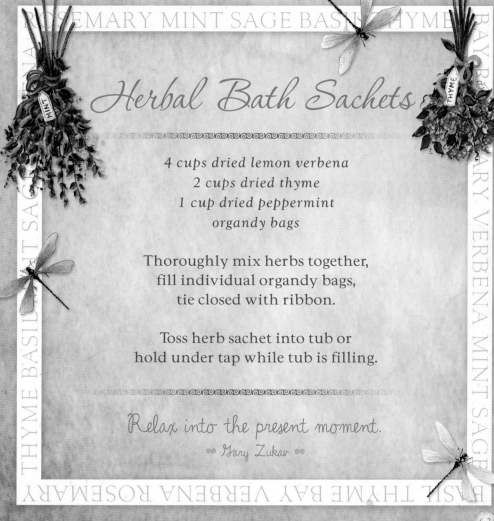

Herbal Bath Sachets

4 cups dried lemon verbena
2 cups dried thyme
1 cup dried peppermint
organdy bags

Thoroughly mix herbs together,
fill individual organdy bags,
tie closed with ribbon.

Toss herb sachet into tub or
hold under tap while tub is filling.

Relax into the present moment.
•• Gary Zukav ••

At the end
of each day,
thank yourself for
just being you.

DR. NANCY SNYDERMAN

refreshed

BAY

SAGE

BASIL

THYME